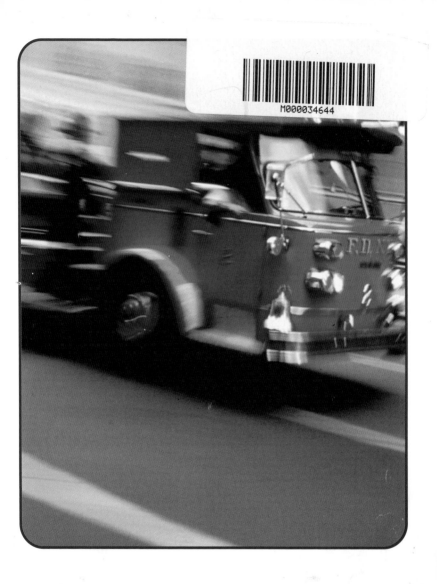

Red, red, this is red.

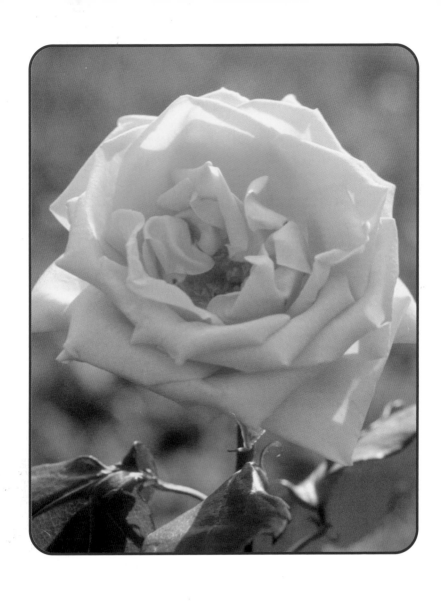

Pink, pink, this is pink.

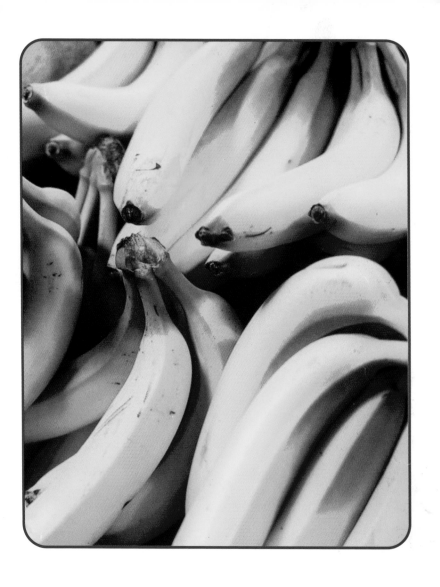

Yellow, yellow, this is yellow.

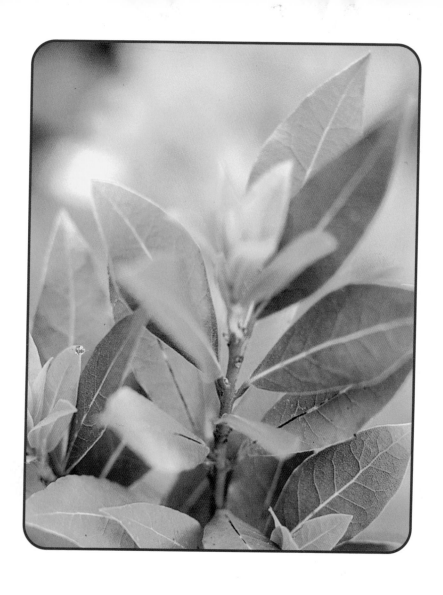

Green, green, this is green.

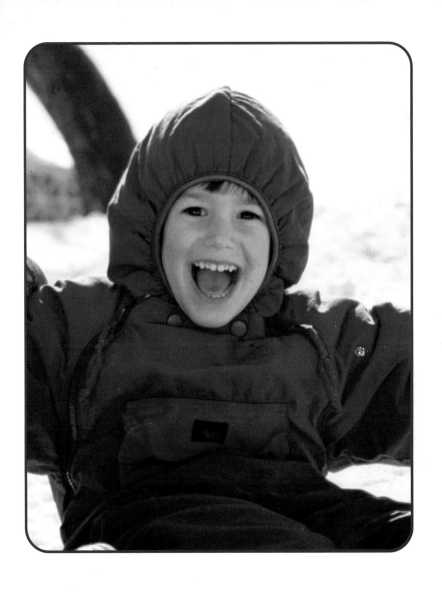

Blue, blue, this is blue.

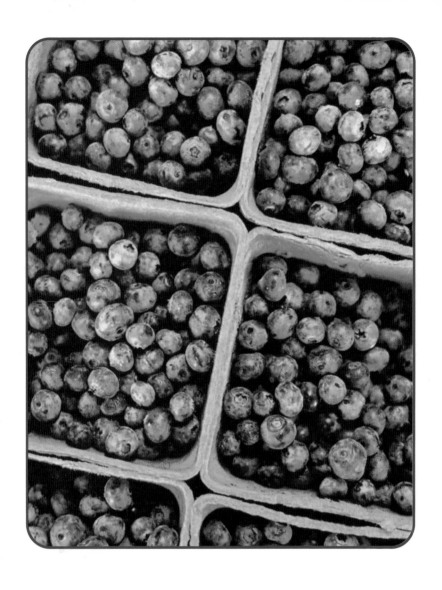

Purple, purple, this is purple.

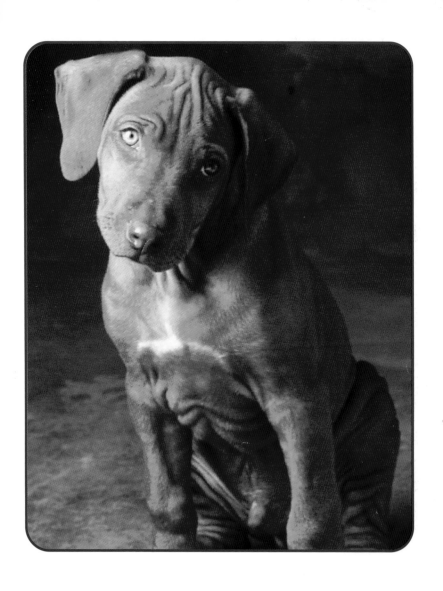

Brown, brown, this is brown.

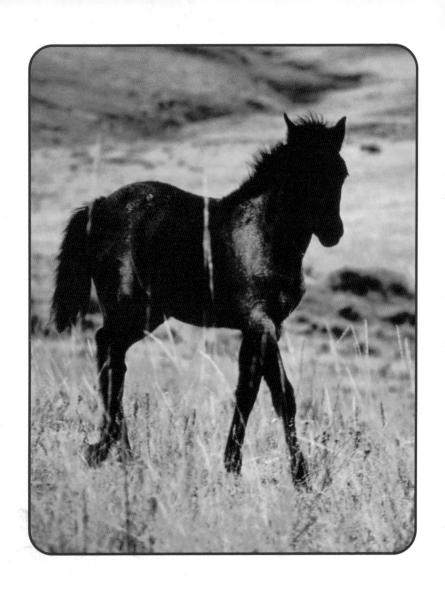

Black, black, this is
black.